To Live Here

To Live Here

Soul Vang

imaginaryfriendpress

Imaginary Friend Press
Copyright © 2014 by Soul Vang

Dan Nowak, editor

Vang, Soul
To Live Here 2014

First edition
ISBN: 978-0-9897395-2-8
Library of Congress Control Number : 2014950083

Cover by Lar Yang
Cover photo by Justin Shell
Interior Design by Sarah Reck

Distributed by Imaginary Friend Press
www.imaginaryfriendpress.com

For my family,
with love.

To The Hmong American Writers' Circle (HAWC).
Thanks for the fellowship,
support,
& encouragement.

Praise for *To Live Here*

Through verses with stunning emotional impact, Soul Vang relates a unique tale of heartbreak, courage, and growth. This is the authentic story of a transplanted culture, told in language of breathtaking beauty and depth.

Margarita Engle, Newbery Honor winner

Among the "elephant poets and philosophers," here in this "land of giants," Soul Vang's voice is a mountain as vast, complex and resilient as the homeland his poems are in perpetual search of. In this startling debut collection, the poet—a once Hmong refugee and U.S. soldier—navigates cultures, languages, geography, and even dreamscapes, with gut-wrenching honesty that is fearless in its probing, and compassionate in its delivery. This is a universal poetry at the height of its powers, a testimony of one man's will and ability to love in the face of his own dispossession. That the community Vang rises out of has only had a written language for some fifty years makes To Live Here an unprecedented and original voice in American letters.

Tim Z. Hernandez, author of *Natural Takeover of Small Things*

To Live Here is a compilation of emotions and stories gathered by a man in love with poetry. Every poem is an expression of his sensitivity to the form; every story is a testament to the strength of memory in remembering feelings and faces in a life full of departure. This is one more addition to the document of the Hmong American experience. Soul Vang has captured the essence of his truth on this road to being Hmong in the world.

Kao Kalia Yang, author of *The Late Homecomer*

"*. . . to form my thoughts/into a glowing message arrow/to transcend the vast night sky*," Soul Vang writes, and this book of poems becomes that arrow, spanning generations and continents, lighting our way, and dismantling some of our most comfortable assumptions. This is a stunning and expansive book of poems. Vang takes us from Laos to Thailand to California, through the violence of war and its aftermath, through gardens and fields and intimate family moments. The poems are spoken with calm and wisdom, and they are filled with love and the nurturing of trees and other growing things, but it is war and loss and displacement that form the difficult heart of the book, making it a profoundly American story. These poems are sung by one who has the will to tell others—unflinchingly and with grace and amazing skill—exactly what he has seen. "*I will have to . . . give/the wind my song*," Vang writes, "*and let all who can,/hear.*" I advise you to listen carefully.

Corrinne Clegg Hales, author of *To Make it Right*

Contents

How Do I Begin?   1

I

Letter from the Shore of the Dragon River   7
The Last Sky   8
Colors   11
The Battle   13
The Old Capital   14
Our Fields   15
Love & War   18
South of the Clouds   19

II

Letter from the Shore of the Dragon River   23
Strange and Familiar Birds   24
Immunization   26
Strays   27
Overheard Advice to New Immigrant   29
Doors   30
Name Change   31
Other Asian   33
Chino   34
My Father   35
Afternoon at the Long Cheng Café   36
To Live Here   38

III

Letter from the Shore of the Dragon River   43
The Special Forces Soldier I Met on the Trail   45
Initiation   47
The Amulet   49
The American   51

Ulenspiegel   54
The Leaving   56
In My Fresno Backyard   58
A Love Poem   59
Second Wind   60
Walking Up and Down the Snowy Hills   61
Shaman Poet   62

IV

Letter from the Shore of the Dragon River   67
My War with Slugs   68
The Hmong Way of Love   70
Lessons   72
Fallen Apple   74
Vision   75
A Tropical Garden in the San Joaquin Valley   76
A Year on the Road   78
Hunger   79
Pool of Youth   81
Drowning   83
Suburban Landscape   84
A Cold Wind   85
Autumn Thoughts   86
Asian Village Walks   87
Late August Day at Mauna Kea Beach   89
Journey to the Central Coast   91
Shelter Cove   93
I Belong There   95
The Last Drops   96
In the End   97
After the Death of General Vang Pao   98

How Do I Begin?

Once, American poets were born
in the factories of Detroit,
the broken plantations of the South,
the vineyards of the Great Valley,
but they were all raised on the plains of Iowa.
They wrote about life enclosed
by picket fences, children creating
kingdoms under apple orchards,
tornadoes turning trees into rows
of corkscrews and carrying trout
miles out of rivers.

Now, here I am, adopted citizen,
not rooted in this land, unable
to taste the spirit in its dust,
to sense its moods in the pollen.
How do I begin my song?
Where do I enter the chorus
when my part is not yet written,
when the conductor won't point
my way?

Shall I start with my birth on Sky Mountain?
Then follow with my childhood,
shaping paper planes to ride the wind?
Or shall I tell of my boyhood,
playing on the shore of the Dragon River
that flowed like a cool blue ribbon in summer
but raged into a churning yellow monster
during monsoon season?

Shall I sing of fleeing
my homeland, knowing I was leaving

the mountains and gorges forever?
Should I sing of crossing
the Mekong, floating on a bamboo raft?
Or sing of my coming to this land as a beggar,
wishing to share my story, but unable
to speak the language?

If I sing of these things,
who would listen to me
who knows nothing of the beauty
of picket fences, the sanctuary
of apple orchards, or the lessons
of tornadoes?

I will have to relearn
and trust my childhood, give
the wind my song
and let all who can,
hear.

I

Monsoon Season

Where should we go after the last frontiers,
where should the birds fly after the last sky?

~ Mahmoud Darwish

Letter from the Shore of the Dragon River

I. *Monsoon Season*

So news of you finally reaches me here
on the shore where we used to run and play.
I heard you had crossed Mekong River
to seek refuge in the land of the Thai.

I heard they put you in a cattle pen
and for a year fed you left-over scraps,
that you lived in shanties of sticks,
drank water from wells dug next to shit holes.

Now they tell me that you have flown
in a metal eagle into the land of giants.
Are they like the stories we heard—
do they feed you till you are fat to eat?

Here on the shore of the Dragon River,
nothing has changed, except for your presence.
The river flows calmly in blue summer
and brings raging yellow monsoon currents.

The Last Sky

The fall of Long Cheng (Sky Base), 1975

Twenty thousand
pairs of eyes
scan the sky
for signs
of lifeboats—C-130s
to rescue us
from *Clear Valley*,
our last fortress
that has become
our deathtrap:
enemy columns surround
the hills,
enemy tanks blockade
the roads,
slowly
moving in
to kill.

Finally,
three American C-130s arrive
like a wing
of birds—three bright eagles
landing, rolling
in a line
up the runway.
The crowd parts
and reforms
like waves
around ships
at sea, scrambling
into
the cargo holds.
Families

try
to stay
together,
but wives
are separated
from
husbands,
children
from
grandparents.

The cargo holds
quickly
filled,
the ramps
start
to rise.
People fall
in clumps
to the hard
tarmac.
An infantry major
grabs
his oldest
son,
boosting
him
into the last gap
of a closing
ramp.

The birds
turn,

roll
down
the Sky Base
runway
for the last
time,
pick up
speed,
lift,
and lumber
into
the last
sky.

Colors

The word "*see*" in Thai has many meanings,
depending on the intonation one uses.

As refugee urchins, we ventured
out of the camp to roam the Thai town
that had become an unwilling host
to an influx of foreign humans
who had settled into their cattle pasture.
They watched us with unease
as we forced the barbed wires
and crawled out to return their curiosity.

One of our favorite activities
was to make the two-mile trek
to the western shore of the Mekong,
gaze east at our homeland,
and wade in the yellow currents
that carry the soil of our mountains.

The old Thai looked at us without expression
from their high porches, their fans slowly
trying to negate the humid winds.
The young girls were nowhere
to be seen—safely hidden, one could
only assume. But the Thai boys,
especially the ones some years older
than us, ventured into the streets
and tried to make conversation, offered us
tamarinds, asked us favors, even tried
to learn some Hmong.

They pointed to the Hmong girls
and asked, "How do you ask for '*see?*'

How do you ask for 'colors?'"
Of course, as twelve-year-old boys, we were not ignorant
of the intricacies of human connections.
We just never assumed
they were asking
what they were asking…

When we finally realized
what they were asking,
we spat out the sweet tamarinds
that had turned sour in our mouths,
and returned to the cattle pasture
behind the barbed wires.

The Battle

It wasn't much of a battle,
just a crowd of people--
men, women, children--yelling, jostling,
running along the barbed-wire fence,
almost like at a bullfight
that happened at New Years.

Two crazy Hmong brothers
had taken out their long knives
and chased some Thai cowherds
as they were herding their cattle
pas the refugee camp in the evening.

Everyone was asking why
they were doing such a foolish thing;
now they and their family
would be deported back
to Laos where they had just escaped
with only their lives.

Apparently, the young men and their wives
had encountered the cowherds
in the woods when they were out
foraging for food and firewood.

No one knew for sure what
happened. The men wouldn't say
as the Thai camp guards came
to round them up,
took them to the Mekong,
and put them in a boat
for the other shore.

The Old Capital

A photograph of Luang Prabang, some years after the fall of Laos

Of the Land-of-a-Million-
Elephants sits still
In time,
Bleaching
In the tropical sun,
Mildewing
In the humid rain.

All the elephants are gone.
The elephant king disappeared
Into a reeducation camp.
Elephant warriors were torn
From the flag,
Along with the pedestal
Of honor
And umbrella
And unity.

Elephant poets, philosophers,
Workers, builders,
Merchants
Fled across rivers,
Over oceans
To settle strange lands
On new continents.

Those left behind
Fled
To the hills,
Blended
Into the mountains.

Our Fields

"Get back our fields!

Drive the Han and the Manchu

out of our fields!"

       This was our battle cry.

Hebei, Bejing…
Sichuan, Guizhou, Hunan, Yunnan…
Xieng Khoung, Long Cheng…
       Our mountains and valleys,
       our cities and towns.
       Our lost fields.

Chiyou…
Ba-yue Wu, Lui-deng Shi, San-bao Shi, Tian-ban Shi…
Xiu-mei Zhang…
Vang Pao…
       Our lost kings and generals.

      ~

Chiyou fought ten battles
for our fields around Beijing.
       He won all
       but the last.

Ba-yue Wu, Lui-deng Shi, San-bao Shi, Tian-ban Shi,
Xiu-mei Zhang fought three wars
for our fields in southern China.
       They lost all three. With each lost,
       we were driven farther

into the southern provinces
where we *Miao* still cling
to barren mountaintops, go hungry
six months out of the year,
drink water from tepid ponds
shared with animals.

Then we were driven into the far mountains
of Vietnam, Burma, Thailand…
And Laos where Vang Pao built the last fortress
at Long Cheng, which we defended for fifteen years,
but, in the end, lost.

Now we Hmong are sowed
to five continents.

~

Argentina, Germany…
Australia, Canada…
United States, France…
            Our new countries.

Fresno, Minneapolis, Stone Mountain, Tampa…
Nimes, Grigny, Toulouse, Orleans…
Strasburg, Gammertingen…
Jahouvey, Regina…
Sydney, Brisbane…
            Our patches of new farmlands,
            vegetable fields, vineyards,
            fruit plantations…
            Our new fields.

Hold on to our new fields!

Dig into our new fields!

Grow in our new fields!

Love & War

Long Cheng, 1972

Midnight,
the general paces
the corridors
of his Motel 6–
like compound,
waiting to see
which wife's door
would open,
which mountaintop
would erupt
so he can scramble
the Ravens,
call for the Sabres,
send in
the Chinooks.

South of the Clouds

Sauropod Dinosaur skeleton found in Yunnan (South of the Clouds)

Under this slate sky, among these ancient fields
That we *Miao* claimed and tried to keep

The *Han* and the *Manchu* from occupying,
Where we fought, bled, died in many battles,

Are buried *Sauropods* that have lain unseen
Under these flood plains for these two hundred

Million years. *Sauropod, Miao, Manchu*
Han, we're all just tiny islands

Among those archipelagos of clouds
Drifting over these wide plains.

II

In the Caverns of Karst

*To live here
one must take air,
but taking air
commits you
to sharing it...*

~ Robert Bly

Letter from the Shore of the Dragon River

II. *In the Caverns of Karst*

From my bedroll in this little corner—
my private space—of the cavern,
I see countless false stars reflect the flame
of my little candle that tries to turn

the gloom of this void into true night.
I sit here and try to form my thoughts
into a glowing messenger arrow
to transcend the vast night sky:

This past season of rain and storms,
monsoon currents turned the Dragon River yellow,
landslides tore the hillsides open
like wounds, our enemies became

our rulers. They overturned heaven
and earth, drove the survivors
into caverns under these limestone
mountains--our houses of karst.

Here in the cool, vast rooms
we share with bats, life is endless
night—the eternal night of the cavern
and the true nights outside that our killers
leave us to roam, and yearn for the day.

Strange and Familiar Birds

Honolulu, Hawaii

I dream of drowning, struggling
to keep my head above water,
in a river so wide, the surface shows
smooth white crests,
like streaking wing feathers
of a giant bird in flight.
I can't imagine such a volume
of water existing, clinging
to the belly of the world.
I have to imagine it as a kin
to the beloved sea of grassland
of my childhood.

I wake to the familiar doves cooing,
roosters crowing. For a moment, I think I am
sleeping on my bamboo bed
in the little hut on the mountaintop
overlooking the sea of elephant grass.
I look forward to waking, running,
hunting quills in the tall grass.

The longer I am awake, however,
the less familiar things become--bed is too soft,
pillow too high, not at all like my lumpy pillow
of folded clothing stuffed in a bag.

Then the sun starts to shine
through the pane of *glass*!
I jump up at the sound of rumbling
cars, of horns marring the morning quiet.
Through the window comes the smell of ripe mangos
tinted with exhaust fumes
and a tinge of sea salt.

The last thing that makes me accept
I am sleeping in a new bed,
living in a new land, is the sound of voices
carrying clip conversations
to my ears—voices I can't understand,
sounds I can't begin to articulate.

Again, the eloquent crowing
of the familiar rooster
mocks my feeble attempt
to sound out
the new tongue.

Immunization

We fled through bamboo forests,
leaving behind beds
littered with belongings,
carrying only a bag of rice,
and a cook pot strapped on top,
Our valuables hidden
in rolled sashes,
children slung across
chests and backs.

We came to the Mekong,
shed our torn sandals,
and entered the river with shreds
of clothing. We floated
on bamboo rafts and plastic tubes,
crossing to a new land.
Our fortunes suddenly turned
worthless paper, ours silver tales
turned deadly anchors.

Finally, we came to this golden land
where mother works days,
father works nights,
and children learn to live
their new life from TV.
How were we to know
that we had come unprepared,
not immunized
for this new land?

Strays

Here, a house with patchy paints,
faded trims revealing layers
of colors, cardboards shoring
the spaces of window panes.
Two half-dead peach trees
sit ungainly in the front yard.

There, a dusty roof with rusty
makeshift gutters tied to the eaves
with fraying ropes. In the over-grown
front yard, shaded by mulberry trees,
a ruptured sofa and old car seats
are arranged around a broken
70s TV set.

Across the street, two burned properties
sit in heaps of trash and litter—lumber,
glass, car parts and tires, furniture, clothing--
the private lives of houses
exposed for all to see.

On this side street, in this unincorporated
part of town, four nameless strays
roam door to door, pausing to sniff
and explore among the decades-
old houses and trailers.

In other parts of town, groomed,
proud, they might even pass for show dogs:
a big black with white throat, stomach,
and haunches; a small lean brown;
a small cat-shaped black; a fluffy,
mid-size white who leads the pack.

In the dusk, a twenty-year-old Hmong man,
hidden behind a two-inch goatee
and long untidy hair, stumbles home.

Overheard Advice to New Immigrant

I. *Overheard Advice to New Immigrant*

You have to be careful with Americans. Sometimes
they say one thing but do another.
They don't believe reincarnation, but
if they're angry, they will punish you
two, even three lifetimes.

They say they trust God, and in court
swear on Him to tell the truth. But
one time a Hmong woman brings joss sticks
and papers to ask Heaven to take the guilty,
and the judge grows very angry—He
throws her out of His court!

II. *Reflections of an Old Hmong Man*

They only sent their best
to our mountains—the tallest,
the straightest nose, the handsomest.

We thought them all gods,
or at least angels. But
when we get here we find
they're all kinds—just
mortals.

Doors

The more years I live
in this new land, the more doors I open
and close behind me:

doors to cramped one-room
apartments, duplexes, houses—
rented, then owned.

The more years I live
in this new land, the more doors I open
and close behind me:

And like the maze of a carnival
fun-house, I may never find
my way back.

Name Change

You try to pronounce my name
but your tongue is a fish
thrashing on a drying riverbed.
It makes a dull *plip-plop*,
not the musical
swish-splash
that calls my soul.
My name comes out of you
dry, twisted, its meaning
mangled.

When you try to write it,
your language can't invoke
my true name
which has the singing music
of the wind playing
on blades
of elephant grass.

Do I want an American name?
Would I like to be Bob?
Tom? James?
Maybe Peter, Paul, or John?

They are fine American names,
but somehow
just not me.
Still, I have to become
a part of this society,
so I'll close my eyes
and pick…

Then again, this is the land
that Franklin and Jefferson created,
that Ali and Monroe
inherited.
It is only fitting
that I should also
reinvent
myself,
my name.

Other Asian

The government sent me a form
that asks what kind of Asian I am:
Chinese, Japanese, Korean,
Filipino, Lao, Thai, Vietnamese,
or Other Asian. I don't know
where to make my mark.

I am tempted to choose
Chinese, for that is the land
of my great ancestors,
and every time I touch
a product Made in China,
it feels as if I am holding
a piece of home.

I can pick Laotian,
for that is the land that created
my earliest memories
and holds my grandfather's
abandoned bones.

I could claim Thai,
for we left my sister's body
buried in those marshy fields
by the Thai shore
of the Mekong.

Yet, truly I don't belong
to any of the included
categories, except for
Other Asian.

Chino

In the aisles of Wal-Mart,
I bumped into a Mexican boy,
maybe six years old. He looked up long at me
in fear, it seemed. Then he put his fingers
on the outside corners of his eyes and pulled
out and up, slanting his eyes.
"Chino! Chino!" he said.
My hand reflexively swung
to wipe out the little superior smile
from the bold brat's face.

But I took hold
of myself. I scrutinized the boy.
His handsome face—a blend
of East and West—was glowing, happy
almost.

I wanted to say to him: *Yes little brother, my eyes*
are slanted, and rather beautifully, I think.
And yes, I am a Chino, and so are you.
My ancestors came from the land that would become China,
and so did yours. My many-times great grandfather and yours,
they probably played and rode
through the vast steppes together as boys. Maybe
they were even cousins, who cried on each other's shoulders
when yours rode east on the land bridge
and mine was left behind.

My Father

I. *A Holiday from War*

Back from a six-month deployment,
just the two of us in a little hut in the fields,
roasting wild chickens and corns
on the red coals.
Then it was time for fairy tales.

II. *Sacrifice*

He enters a convenience store,
looks at the prices of snacks and drinks,
thinks of his children--their school costs,
their bride prices and dowries, his own funeral.
He exits without buying,
thirsty, full.

III. *Revelation*

Looking at old photographs,
I am already older than him.
Yet I'll always be
his child.

Afternoon at the Long Cheng Café

I inhale the aroma of *fawm*,
prepared the way we Hmong prefer:
thin noodles in steaming clear broth
with slices of beef, chicken, and crispy pork
spiced with green onions and cilantro.
I look out the window and I don't see
Kings Canyon Boulevard, nor the Ferris wheel
and carnival lights of the Big Fresno Fair
across the street.

Rather, my senses turn inward
and I remember the first time
I had eaten *Fawm Looj Ceeb*
at the original Long Cheng Café,
a block from General Vang Pao's compound:

It is a special treat from mother,
for I have come to visit from the relative peace
of the country village
where I have been left with an uncle
to continue my schooling, away
from the artillery shelling
that increasingly interrupts
the daily life of Long Cheng.

Mother and I sit in the Long Cheng Café
to avoid a light afternoon shower,
enjoy a bowl of fawm,
and watch the throng crowding the roadway
that wends through roadside shops
and food stands serving busy housewives,
soldiers, and swaggering Hmong pilots
who have just found the power

and prestige of being able to fly
like gods. Children escape the clutches
of their mothers and chase one another
past gawking American pilots
and military advisors...

Army jeeps splash through the wet, winding road
paved with crushed karst rocks
shining like diamonds in the afternoon sun.

To Live Here

Oakland, California

Among these skyrises
& screeching cars,
these crowded lanes
& sculpted parks,
one must take air,
but taking air commits you
to sharing it
with:

The Korean woman
& her Sikh boyfriend
enjoying a profusion of dishes
at Jonga House;

The African-American man
& his Chinese wife
walking protectively around her elderly parents
along Grand Avenue;

The laughing Latina high-schooler
& her poly-ethnic friends
offering you
their unneeded bus transfers;

The ducks
& the geese
floating gently in a line
across Lake Merritt;

The sturgeons
& the stripers
living in dark waters under the fishing pier
jutting from the embarcadero,

on which is attached a sign
warning of health risks
in seven languages.

III

Sky Soldier on a Mountaintop

*I returned home,
a big-game hunter
of emotions.*

~ Yehuda Amichai

Letter from the Shore of the Dragon River

III. *Sky Soldier on a Mountaintop*

From among the leafy banana field,
I pressed warm metal trigger, raising
death among the enemy camp
just as they sat down to lunch.

When the enemy came to burn us out of the caverns
where we had taken refuge, I escaped here to join
the Sky Soldiers, hoping their holy rituals of invincibility
would protect me as I learned to kill.

Today, I squeezed off hundreds of rounds,
as easily as dropping beads of sweat.
I am a wise old man at fifteen,
knowing death is nothing.

On the hilltop that is the enemy's
compound, frenzy and confusion reigned.
Our bullets hit some, but most
died from their own blind artillery.

The sound of their cries, interrupted
by artillery rounds, was at first chilling.
But the farther we ran, the less distinct
they became—they could be mistaken
for cries of joy.

It's almost dark now as I sit here
on the top of our mountain and watch
them come to gather their dead
and carry them off like ants
trailing back to their nests.

I sit here and watch the Dragon River curve
like a silver ribbon towards you and the setting sun,
smell the sweet odor of burnt flesh,
and wait for the wind to turn.

The *Special Forces* Soldier I Met on the Trail

Army Basic Training, Fort Jackson, South Carolina

It was the fifth or sixth week, after we had gotten in the groove,
after we had been structured in routines: PT before dawn,

rifle-range in midmorning, warfare classes in afternoon.
Then we ran the obstacle course through a dense jungle

that reminded me so much of the home I had left as a child eight
       years earlier.
My training buddy & I sped through the trail, only pausing to crawl

under barbed-wire nets, vault fallen logs—"a walk in the jungle" for
       me,
swing across pits of brown water, scale up

& scramble down walls. Suddenly we came to an obstacle
astride the trail; I forget what station it was: rope swing or wooden
       wall.

What I remember is the *Special Forces* soldier monitoring the
       obstacle--
Lanky, stoop-shouldered, maroon beret pulled low

over his face, sergeant's chevrons & *Special Forces* tab adorned
his olive uniform. His eyes opened wide in shock when he saw me.

"Where are *you* from?" he demanded.
"Laos," I perplexedly replied.

And he nodded knowingly, as if he had only asked to confirm.
"*You* know where it is?" my buddy asked.

"Yes," he said softly, "*another* country *we* invaded!"

Only as the years passed, have I come to understand
his enigmatic statement. He must have seen hundreds,

thousands like me when he was a White Star, sent to my far jungle
to train my fathers & older brothers how to hold a gun,

to strip & reassemble a weapon, to lay a field of fire,
to set tripwires & camouflage Claymores, to kill with efficiency,

to die. I was a ghost, trailing his guilt to find him at last
in the midst of his American jungle.

Initiation

Rivers Army Barrack; Giessen, Germany

My first evening at Rivers Barracks,
I visit the base club--a low building
hiding in a corner of the compound,
behind the little chapel, past the motorpool
full of trucks and artillery pieces.
As I walk in, a blast of Garth Brooks greets me.
On the dance floor, two women
are wobbling country steps.
To the right, leaning on the bar,
are some white guys in cowboy attires
and some black men in their best suits
and long leather jackets.

They all turn to look at me,
like an audience focusing
on the stage.
A black man in his thirties walks over,
taking his time, boldly
looks down at me, then asks:
"Where you from?"
"California!" I reply proudly.
"No! I mean where are you from,
Originally!"

I pause.

"Africa!"

"Hey, are you messing with me?" the man asks,
voice rising. I almost back down.
"No, man. If I were, you would know it.
Besides, you're not that good looking."
It seems the appropriate cliché,

something right
out of a movie scene.

He foams at the mouth.
His breath is a rushing storm of whisky vapor.
"You little Chink!
I know you're not from Africa.
I'll show you to mess with me."

"Hey, I'm serious.
It was a complete surprise to me, too,
when they told me in school that all people
originally came out of Africa.
And you did ask where I am from,
Originally!"

He looks at me. I look at him.

"You new?" he finally asks.
"Yeah, just got in this afternoon."
"Hey, you're okay, man. Foolish, but okay.
Come over to the bar, brother from Africa!"

The Amulet

When I entered the army,
father bequeathed me an amulet
of proven power--he had worn it
and survived a fifteen-year war.

I grew up hearing tales of father
always walking point
but never being hit,
while others fell left, right, or behind him.
One time he vaulted a trench
into an enemy hilltop, threw three grenades
into three bunkers, vaulted another bend
of the trench and was gone,
leaving the enemy dead in their sleep.

The amulet was a curious
sliver of silver, a small ax blade.
"This is a thunder ax,"
he told me. "I found it in a tree
fell by lightning.
It will protect you
as it has protected me."

I took the amulet like a Christmas present,
stowed it in my backpack, and went off
to join the U. S. Seventh Army in Germany.
On a trip to Amsterdam, my buddies and I roamed
the red light district all night, only to return
to a looted car—all belongings gone.

So father's amulet is protecting
some fortunate Dutch
in that city where one desperately

needs protection.
Or it could be lying
at the bottom of a canal,
protecting the city.

The American

In the quiet shades of the evening,
a cool Atlantic wind blows,
bringing a hint of salt,
dispersing the long day of summer heat.
I take a break from the marching
boots in snap-steps, shining
like flashing mirrors, uniforms
spit-shined with colors—gold,
red, white, blue—paraded in a field
of green, among perfect rows
of white crosses clouding
the rolling hills, decorated
with American flags. I stroll
in the middle of a little Belgian town
that has seen American GIs
come on their yearly pilgrimage
of salute to these holy hills
where their comrades had fallen
in two world wars.

I, however, out of uniform,
must be something they don't quite expect
in an American—not Johnson Blonde,
Varnado Black, or even Chavez Brown.
I can pass for a World War II Japanese,
I could be a Chinese who has come
to open a restaurant, maybe even
a Vietnamese refugee escaping by boat
from his homeland to seek shelter in France
or here in Belgium.

The old lady, closing the door to her jewelry
shop, doesn't know what to make of me. But

she greets me tentatively in English,
and asks where I'm from.
"The U.S.," I answer. She pauses. "Oh!
You must be with the American soldiers."
When I answer "Yes," she is happy.
"We were at the ceremony today."

She invites me in, to a room in the back
of the shop--hidden, a secret chamber
for resistance fighters, spies,
soldiers downed behind enemy lines.
I am ushered to a hearth
surrounded by three old couples
enjoying their memories,
revived with a flickering fire,
fresh cookies, and good coffee.
They greet me with smiles
and invite me to a seat in their circle.

They have an American friend, they tell me,
whom they visit yearly in Pennsylvania.
Their friend had been a pilot,
shot down, wounded, lost and helpless,
until rescued by these people,
who must have been young lovers then,
filled with the juices of fighting
for their lives.

They welcome me, I think, as a brethren
of their American friend. I accept
their extended grace, the warmth
of their fire. I don't mind
when I think of my many American years,

exploring strip malls, supermarkets,
department stores, without
ever seeing an American hearth
or tasting homemade apple pie.

I tell them my American story
of being born on Sky Mountain, fleeing
across the Mekong, living
in the refugee camp, coming
to America, joining
the United States
Army.

Ulenspiegel

Giessen, Germany

I strayed from the main
street-mall in downtown Giessen,
ambled through a narrow lane
between tall buildings,
and emerged in a beergarten
that led to a door
with the faded name: *Ulenspiegel*

Steps led down to a bunker--
a half-sphere room,
decorated with black and white,
life-size photos of 1950s movie stars.
Bogart, Bacall, Bergman,
and Cooper gazed
down at the patrons.
A fireplace warmed
the far end of the room.
The bar hugged the right wall;
a door to the left led
to a cozy dance hall.

The weissen beer was cold,
soothing; the music: jazz smooth.

I gradually stopped frequenting
hard rock cafes and discothèques,
and became a regular
at *Ulenspiegel*--
along with a self-exiled gay
African American opera singer
from Georgia, a Canadian exchanged
student who never returned
to Canada, a bankrupted playboy

from England who had lost
his fortune but never
his class, a half-American
half-German army brat
from California.

Being an exiled
Hmong from Laos
and adopted American,
I felt a part
of the cast.

The Leaving

"Friendly fire" and "Death
by enemy hand" are common.
But there are also obscure ways
one leaves the army.

Johnson, riding shotgun
in a Hummer one night
in a black-out driving exercise,
is cut in half by the nose
of a parked Abrams tank.

Whitman, bespectacled target
of taunts and torments,
vaults the compound fence,
runs head-on into a semi
on the autobahn.

Demby, initiated into
a group of resentful
black soldiers--mugging,
vandalizing, stealing--
is turned in by an undercover
black brother.

My time is up, so I pack quietly
on this Friday night, when friends
are out numbing their suffering
in the clubs and pubs.
In the brightening dawn, I quietly
board the shuttle to the airport
for the trip back to the "world."

In the army, the dead
and the leaving
are brothers.
New people arrive
and old ones quietly
disappear with the dawns.

Except for Demby, who whispered:
"Good bye, Cool Breeze!"
that early dawn they took him. I replied
in a whisper, not wanting
to wake others.

In My Fresno Backyard

The *Asics* sneaker hangs awkwardly
on the branch, next to ripe peaches.
It's a formless clump, almost
unidentifiable. Its once-shiny purple
racing stripes are torn
and meshed into the dried mud.
Looking at it, it's hard to imagine
that sneaker and its missing mate
once belonged to the Six-Hundred-Mile Club
of the U.S. Seventh Army in Europe.
They trotted those hundreds of miles together,
eating the grainy soil of Germany.
They explored old castles
and stepped on the toes
of centuries-old ghosts.
They walked on the rubble of the citizen-demolished
Berlin Wall, feeling the sharp ruins of an idea
still trying to prick through their soles.
They stepped over the torn curtain of iron
that had turned velvet
and ran a marathon through the worn
cobblestone streets of Prague,
where the people had found
renewed vision in the Russian tanks
painted by vandal citizens
in laughing pink.
They even traveled to Auschwitz, Poland,
where all the participants are gone, but
where one side's power lingers
and the other's will remains—
in the piles of hair clippings
and mounds of shoes
refusing to rot.

A Love Poem

for May

Walking along Sunset Beach,
The direction hardly matters.
The endless sand stretches
North to Alaska, south to Argentina.

Cypresses and Sequoias guard the coast
As children shout in unaccustomed joy--
A rare outing at the beach.

Footprints and dog tracks travel
Side-by-side, as an English Setter protects
A family and a Shih Tzu keeps
An old man company.

Northern Harriers and Kingfishers fly low
Over the surf to compete with a fisherman
Who has cast his lure into the waves.

The tide recedes to reveal two rocks
Pounded smooth by the waves.
I look to the east
And think of you.

Second Wind

A paper plane, abandoned
by neighborhood kids
on the hood of my secondhand
Datsun 280Z, became wet in the drizzle,
matted itself onto the white,
painted steel. I left it there to dry
and rest its wings
as I folded my
35-year-old body
into the seat
and traveled my daily miles
to school.
Racing with me at 70 mph north
on freeway 41,
the plane lifted
and flew up the embankment
over the hedge
that hugs the freeway,
over apartments and houses,
malls and mansions,
farms and ranches,
surfing the wind
towards the Sierra Nevada.

Walking Up and Down the Snowy Hills

Phoenix Lake; Sonora, California

Waking up to the first snow of the season,
We take a walk among the undulating hills

Overlooking Phoenix Lake--spreading out
Like a jagged silver star below.

We enjoy the soft crunch underfoot,
Marvel at pine branches cradling precious crystals.

We touch the snow-dusted fruits of the manzanita,
Taste the tangy berries that look so similar

To the salty *txiv huabtxhib* we ate on the humid hills
Of far Laos. We wonder:

How does one compare the fruits
Of two such different lands?

Shaman Poet

The poet relies on his faith
in English and calls words out of random air
with an intuitive knowledge
that the word he needs
will scroll next on the page.

He calls one to soothe, one to meditate,
one to proclaim, one to challenge...

The shaman sings chants long memorized
and have become a part of him
as he calls spirit guides to aid his journey
to soothe and retrieve lost souls,
negotiate with recalcitrant spirits,
battle evil demons.

He calls one to guide, one to conduct etiquettes,
one to be his shield, one to be his lance...

How sad for the modern Hmong poet
who has no shaman calling
and for the old Hmong shaman who can't master
the new language.

The poet—a successor who can't inherit. The shaman—
a master without apprentice.

What a *shaman poet* would be like—
singing old chants and creating new songs,
calling spirits, negotiating, fighting demons
old and new, in both Hmong and English—

We can only imagine.

IV

In the Jungle

*What do I know
of redemption or sacrifice,
what will I have to say
of the dead?*

~ Brian Turner

Letter from the Shore of the Dragon River

IV. *In the Jungle*

I have only twelve bullets,
one for each approaching man.
Aim for the chest,
one stops and clutches
the red patch spreading.
Aim for the head,
another drops like a full sack.
Then comes the Cuban Advisor—
a dark giant half again as tall as the men
he leads, with arms big as thighs,
rushing at me with double pistols.
A shot to the chest only makes him flinch;
a belly shot only makes him pause.
It takes nine bullets,
from groin to neck,
to drop him in front of me.
I am surprised to see how young,
how surprised he is to be
dying in this dense jungle so far
from his tropical island
home.

My War with Slugs

Sunshine, my one-year-old daughter,
ate a slug one day. I only found out
when she hit her chin on the windowsill,
bit her lower lip, and began to cry in shock
as she spewed blood, curdled milk, food—and
a piece of strange-looking
material—onto my shirt.
I rubbed the thing between my fingers
and felt its slimy skin. When I squeezed,
out came its sticky intestines.

Since then I have been on a personal crusade
against those creatures of the dark
and damp crevices of the earth.
I flooded their homes in the flowerbeds
and sprinkled salts on them
when they climbed up the walls or onto rocks.
They turned an amber color and began to foam
in their death spasms.

When the salt couldn't keep up
with their numbers, I sprayed them
with foamy wheel cleaner. The smell
swarmed through the house.
My wife complained bitterly. I didn't listen;
I kept spraying, watching slugs freeze and die.

I thought I had won the war;
it'd been a while since I have seen any slugs.
Little did I know that they have gone
underground—in preparation for a full-scale assault.
Today, I found them creeping en masse
from under the walls into the spare room

that I had planned to be the babies' room.

They seem to anticipate me.
They must have spies somewhere—
maybe inside me. Who knows, I could have
eaten a slug when I was a baby. And now it's there,
living near my heart, conspiring.

The Hmong Way of Love

I love you!
You are doing a great job!
This is the way you do it... That's right... There you go... Great!

These were all foreign
concepts of expression
that we Hmong had to learn
in this new land, as foreign
as eating bread,
going to the mall, seeing
the ocean.

My father used to whip me for my transgressions.
My mother would scold me for my mistakes.
Then afterwards they would tell me:
I only hit/scold you because I care
about you. If I didn't care, I wouldn't bother at all, wouldn't say
anything no matter what you do.
So I learned not to do many things
that I knew were wrong,
as well as things I feared
might be wrong.

The Hmong way of love was
a bit like poetry: it used a lot of figurative language and
symbolic gestures,
and you had to interpret layers
of words and actions
to find the intent.

The Hmong way of love is
changing: poetry blending
with prose. So that our daughters

and sons may learn
what not to do;
but more importantly,
what to do
and why.

Lessons

from my daughters

What a tough taskmaster you are
to constantly test my vigilance,
my sincerity, my worth
as a father, as a person.
How persistent you are
in your task, how creatively
innovative your tests.
You must have graduated
from a great school, learned
from a great teacher.

All your lessons I keep
repeating in my head
to make sure I do it right
the next time: I will never again
slam a car door without looking
to see if your fingers
are holding onto the frame.
I will never turn my back on you
and walk away
while you are bouncing on the bed
or sitting on a high chair, for I know
you will jump into the air
to follow me. I will never again
say the evil things surging
out of my heart, for I know
you will be repeating
those same words
back to me in a humorous tone.
I will never leave you
unsupervised outside,
for I know you will rush
headlong into the street

squealing and daring me to catch you.
I will never make a move
without watching myself,
whether to dance,
to slap, to stroke,
or to fly,
for I know
you will master it soon
and, with delight,
repeat it to me.

Fallen Apple

I. *Fallen Apple*

My three-year-old son finds a fallen apple.
With his toy shovel, he digs a little hole
in the flowerbed, places the apple snugly in,
then piles on a mound of dirt, and soon
the apple is gone.

How does he know
that the apple prefers the kind
embrace of the moist soil
to drying in the sun?

II. *The Deaf Man*

points at his own ear
and signs me a thumb-down,
he points at his head
and signs me a thumb-up.

He then points at the head
of the autistic child
I hold in my arms
and gives me a thumb-down.

All I can give him
is a smile.

III. *Body Found*

in Canal Where Autistic Boy
Disappeared
Another headline:
Autistic Teen Scores 20
in Basketball Game

Vision

I walked off Warmerdam Field
one spring morning two years ago
after a four-mile run.
The sun had just climbed
a hand's width into the sky.

A woman who had already
been running when I arrived
was still running, her walking cane
tinking, tinking against the metal
rail that curves along the inside lane.

After two years of sweet living,
accumulating thirty pounds of love
handles from luxurious loving,
after fathering one child and anxiously
awaiting the arrival of another,

I have come back to Warmerdam Field
on this drizzly Autumn morning
to shed the sweetness of life
that has lately been cloying.
And the running woman's still here:

running in her same blue shorts, white shirt,
and red hat that covers hair neatly
pulled into a ponytail. Every four steps,
her cane taps the metal
rail that hedges the grass field.

A Tropical Garden in the San Joaquin Valley

In the Fresno backyard of my subdivision home,
enclosed by block and wood fencing,
in the little yardage of compacted rocky dirt
I co-own with my wife
and the 1st American Mortgage Co.,
I attempt to recreate a place
that would comfort the child
who continues to live
within me, who has grown more estranged
and withdrawn
with each new day
that I attempt to make my way
into this society.
I try to quiet the child, to calm his fears
with the sounds that used to lull him to sleep—
the whistling of tropical leaves in the wind.
So I plant bananas, papayas,
guava, mango, bamboo,
lemon grass, elephant grass...

They struggle to live
as I scramble to save
and nurture them in this foreign soil,
but the mango died in the summer
heat and the guava died
from the winter freeze.
What remains is a patchy semblance
of the landscape the child was born into,
but it has made him more than happy
to see some things so comfortingly
familiar, to hear the lullaby of tropical leaves
played by a worldly wind.

The child is so easy to please,
so innocent, unaware
of the rumbling of traffic,
of trucks and cars passing
at 65 mph,
just over the block
fence.

A Year on the Road

I.

A California bald eagle played chicken
With me at 75 mph. His outspread
Silver-streaked wings blotted
My windshield, his claws clutching
A field mouse. Luckily, his reaction
Was faster than mine—at the last second
He spun into the rising sun.

II.

A red Ram pickup chased me
For two, three miles
On the freeway for
Cutting him off. It was
A confrontation of eyes glaring, hands
Gesticulating, horns blaring,
Tires screeching—two modern knights
At the wrong venue.

III.

A careless car, changing lanes,
Just missed swiping
My rear, lost control, plowed
Through the median bushes
Into opposite lanes, crashed
Head-on into
Oncoming cars—I saw it all
In the rearview
Mirror.

Hunger

At a time of the evening
when most families are sitting
around the table for dinner,
I am just leaving for
my second job,
teaching struggling college students
how to organize their thoughts
on paper.

At the crossroads
of Shields and Blackstone,
I meet the eyes
of two young men
stationed at opposite sides of the street.

One man is sitting hunched over
a battered blue ice box,
wearing discolored green parka
and black skullcap over oily brown hair.
He has a pack on his back,
a duffel bag at his side,
looking ready to start a long journey,
carrying a sign:
Hungry! Please Help!

The other man is walking briskly
up and down the street,
wearing white T-shirt and black jeans.
His eyes roam the faces
of the drivers stopped at the red light,
hoping to trade the dozen roses
he clutches in his hand
for a few dollars.

His unkempt black hair,
his lean brown face
speak of his arrival from a long journey
through tunnels under fences,
through military live-firing ranges,
through deserts and strange towns,
crossing borders.

Pool of Youth

During the warm evenings of August,
the high school pool was full;
Up to forty people crowed the lanes,
swimming laps to stay fit.
Through the cooling evenings of September,
the sun began to set earlier.
Some swimmers dropped off;
a few new ones appeared.
The floodlights were turned on in October,
and they magnified the stars
and the half-moon swimming
across the night sky.
In the cold November evenings,
rains began to fall.
Thunder and lightning sometimes
chased us from the pool.
"You'll love swimming in the rain,"
Doug said. He was right.
There is nothing quite like swimming
in a warm pool with cool rain drops
playing on your back and your face
as you turn to take in a breath.
By December, there were only seven of us,
each swimming in his own lane.
Steams rose in tendrils,
as if they were extensions of the ripples
on the surface of the pool.
We each occupied our own world,
walled in by the luminous fog,
only occasionally glimpsing a neighbor
passing in the next lane.
Ike, who had swum in the lane
next to mine all semester, told me

more of his story.
"I was born here in Clovis," he said.
"There were only two thousand people then;
now it's eighty thousand.
I fought the Japanese in the Burma Theater,"
said the robust, eighty-five year-old Japanese American,
whom I'd mistakenly thought to be about sixty.
"I've been swimming for two years,"
said Doug, another neighbor
who has the physique of an Olympian.
"I'd been injured in a motorcycle accident
and couldn't workout any other way."
"Steve, Ike, and coach have been swimming
since the beginning," said Noah.
Steve is a triathlete in his forties.
No one knows how old coach Roycelyn is.
She could be any age
between twenty and thirty-five.
"We've been doing this for twenty years,"
she told me the first day I joined them.

Drowning

The gravity of the water enfolds me like a warm death
as I sprint the last four laps to cap the night's swim.
From below, the surface is a windowpane that protects
and holds the swimmer in an underworld from the bullets
of rain that shatter against the clear plane.

Every muscle in my body aches for rest, for stillness.
My mouth grasps for air from one stroke to the next.
My lungs are about to collapse in the next heartbeat.
This is how my father must have felt

as they pulled the breathing tube from his mouth,
as he gasped for air and fought with every muscle
of his body to live till the next heartbeat,
to suck in the next precious breath.

He fought for an hour, and through the whole time
I was thinking: This is a mistake; he isn't dead.
But it was already too late. I had given my consent
when the medical resident pulled me aside
and informed me my father was dead
and was only breathing because of the machine.

Suburban Landscape

I. *Frontyard Boundaries*

Leaves from the neighbor's tulip trees
litter my lawn, crackling across the driveway,
crumbling underfoot.

By the front door, the galaxy magnolia
bares her limbs like a bride
reluctantly shedding her gown.

The plumerias--blooming pink and white--
will have to be moved under the eaves
to avoid frost.

II. *Backyard Garden*

Bees collect the last nectars
from the flowering vegetables;
pumpkins harvested, vines composted.

At the first strong wind,
the browning peach leaves plummet
like a flock of sparrows.

The redwood gazebo
will have to be stained
and sealed against rain.

A Cold Wind

Ruffles branches of trees guarding the backyard.
Bamboo leaves hum softly with the wind.

Perched on a light pole, a lone sparrow
courageously chirps to hold back autumn.

Beyond the brick wall, morning traffic reverberates.
Overhead a silver plane heads northwest;

Its shape--an arrow piercing the underbelly
of earthy clumps of clouds trying to hide

blue sky above. Old people claim
they can feel the change of seasons

in their aching bones. That's something
at least I don't yet feel.

Autumn Thoughts

after Du Fu

No sound of birds singing; they've migrated
on the sky road to warmer climes,

leaving us mortals behind.
The first green olives turn dark.

Persimmons ripen on the bough;
pomegranate seeds grow so full

they burst the red rinds, allowing ants
and spiders to reach the red, tart juice.

The first drops of autumn rain
splatter my picture windows,

and I'm glad my Saturday chores are done.
I've spent all day trimming trees, weeding flowerbeds,

sweeping the crumbly leaves of the neighbor's
tulip trees that litter my driveway.

Already, another year passes,
and I've done nothing noteworthy.

Asian Village **Walks**

for G Man

Crank: A light name for a serious man,
son of an itinerant preacher--a trouble-shooter
who took his family on the road
from little town to little town, across states,
to take over failing churches and raise them up again.
The son seems to have inherited the spirit
of the father, still traveling, still setting down
new roots...

Crank: Stocky, short blond hair slicked back,
a blocky jaw, a ready smile, a booming tenor—
a good colleague, a perfect walking partner
with a hello, a how-do-you-do, to everyone
we met among these blocks of shifting tides:
Whites to Mexicans to Hmong back to Mexicans.

Crank and I often walked south along Winery
across Kings Canyon Boulevard,
by the Home Depot that replaced the dilapidated old K-Mart
which for years was a haunted
playground for local kids,
around the well-churned soccer fields,
back through the Food Maxx parking lot
with its dwindling customers.

Or we walked west along Kings Canyon, by Ernie's Bakery
whose windows have displayed Mexican pastries "since 1962,"
pass the old-style barber shop where a red, white and blue
barber's pole still revolves by the front door,
around the corner where the closed Ritmo Latino stands
surrounded by numerous thriving pay day loans,
to the new Olmos Elementary school,
built where demolished homes once stood.

But our favorite route was east
through the Creekside apartments,
across Willow, through a block of old ranch houses
where the last white man on the block strolls
among his shady oaks and lush grapevines,
looking conspicuous next to the immigrant yards
with their groves of bamboos and bananas,
to Trolley Creek Park with its Victorian gables
and graffitied sidewalks that testify
to new stakes being claimed.

Only now that Crank has moved on,
only now as I am walking alone
along these shifting routes, do I feel the discomfort,
when my mumbled hellos and how-do-you-dos
to the occasional elderly white lady, the Mexican teen-ager, the
          African-American man
go unanswered or returned with a suspicious look,
do I realize that it may take years--
maybe generations--
for me, a Hmong man, to walk here
with the confidence and ease
of Crank.

Late August Day at Mauna Kea Beach

Big Island, Hawaii

Perfect morning:
sugary sand,
sparse crowd,
warm sun.

In afternoon,
grow restless,
leave the wife
slumbering,
take a trail
across rugged headland
of sharp volcanic lava.

Meet two old men
carefully negotiating trail,
one who obviously had suffered
a stroke—
one leg stiff, one hand
clutches close to chest.
Make way for them
and ask
how far still to go.

"You're about
half way there."

Farther, come across
a site of old native settlement:
house foundations, stone rings
for cooking.
Encroaching, just yards up the slope,
red-tile-roofed villas

with horizontal pools—the kind that blends
with sea and sky
when one looks from the porch.

In the rocky inlets,
sea turtles glide,
almost flying,
in their element,
elemental.
Their cold-blooded bodies cradled
by the currents
of warm blue sea.
They worry not
about lost civilizations,
current occupations,
the end of worlds.

Journey to the Central Coast

Starting out late, we face the sunset
As we leave the plains behind.
The road climbs the coastal range,
Hugging slopes, snaking between peaks
Onto the highland moor.

The sky ahead turns
From red, to orange, to indigo
As we cross York Road,
Almond Road, then Bitterwater Road.
Lights from lonely ranch houses
Twinkle in the distance.
Cattle sleep in dark clumps
Amidst brown fields.
Road signs warn of high winds
And dust storms.

As the sky darkens to match
The darkling earth, our only guides
Are a solid white line to the right
And a broken yellow line
To the left. Our only company,
The haunting melodies of Teresa Teng—
The words we don't understand, but
The music perfectly echoes
The curves of this lonely road.

Cocooned in the cab of the Tundra,
It seems we've been traveling
This dark road forever and are destined
To travel it evermore.
I doze off momentarily, shake
Myself awake, and am not sure

If I'm leaving
Or returning.

Shelter Cove

As sun descends to meet watery horizon,
its reflection is a shimmering road of gold
bridging the edge of the world
to the hidden cove below.

We stand in a lacquered gazebo
on a cliff isle that is only reached
by an arching stone bridge
that spans an ever-widening breach
created by forces of winds and waves.

The isle has been drifting and falling
from land since before Spaniards
and their missions,
before Chumas times, maybe
even before dinosaurs
lived in caverns at the cliff base.

From the cliff-top gazebo, we breathe in
the panorama of the sea scene.
Besides us, the only living things are birds
in their crags, squirrels in their burrows,
and a lone fir tree.

On the tree trunk, someone has left
attached a bouquet of red
and white plastic roses

in memory of some loved one,
who, by accident
or intent, had slipped
down the sheer cliff
to meet the rocky cove,

in memory of these birds
and squirrels with their brief lives,
in memory of us standing here
who will someday fall
to the cove below
and travel that shimmering road,

in memory of this fir tree
and this cliff isle
that will someday crumble
into the sea,

in memory of this shelter earth
that someday will be nothing
but a golden shimmer
of dust in this dark universe.

I Belong There

after Mahmoud Darwish

I belong there. I have many memories.
I was born on Sky Mountain, grew up running on a plain
of elephant grass, nourished by fields that quilted the mountainsides.
I have courtship songs and laughter rising from the fields
to be snatched by a bright eagle surfing the wind.
I have a saturated meadow where I drank dewdrops on banana leaves,
plucked cherries by the roadside, pulled tender shoots from the
                eternal bamboo grove,
scooped fish from the river, harvested mushrooms from the moist
                earth.
The mountain belonged to everyone.
The valley belonged to no one.

I had lived on the land long before brothers rose to overthrow
                brothers,
the victors promising to share the land.

Now the valley is deserted.
The mountain is forbidden.
The meadow is dry: banana, cherry, bamboo trees cut down
and sold to foreign lands, crows pick on the bones
of dead fish on the dry riverbed,
mushrooms won't grow in the parched earth.
People are driven from the mountains
to settle along the roads. Songs fill the dance halls
where young girls throng to entertain travelers and returned Hmong
while local young men look on with empty eyes.

When I finally return to Sky Mountain
on my sky steed, descending like a bright eagle out of the west,
will I feel I have returned
home?

I don't belong there. I have many memories.

The Last Drops

Years ago, we ignored the old men
who gathered when there was a feast
or funeral
and regaled any who would listen
with their tales of war
and conquests
back in the mountains.

Now, when we gather,
the old men are hard to find.
Two or three hide in the corners
and still whisper
their old tales.

Those who know
ignore discussions of jobs,
BMWs, games
of golf, trips
to Thailand
or Laos…
and gravitate to the corners
to drink the last drops
of a mountain spring
running
dry
.

In the End

for Chayut

"In the end,
we'll lose all the things,
language,
traditions,
even our children (when
they are no longer
Hmong),"
you, my friend,
said.

And I think
you're right. But
in the end, we'll
probably never
know.

And are our language,
traditions,
and children
ours to lose,
or just ours to celebrate
and let go?

In the end, all we may
be able to do
is to present
our very best.
And let the next
take it over.

That's what every generation
must have finally felt
and done
in the end.

After the Death of General Vang Pao

Spring, 2011

We wake from our winter
To find spring arrived and settled

~

New vines and leaves sprout
From grape spurs

Peach and pear trees full
Of sudden blossoms

Poppies quilt hillsides
In bright patches

~

Mantles of oranges reduced
To a few golden fruits

The dead sequoia is gone--
Sawed and uprooted

The earth raked smooth
As if nothing had ever been there.

Acknowledgements

Grateful acknowledgement is made to the following publications & anthologies in which these poems appeared, sometimes in slightly different forms.

How Do I Begin? An Anthology of Hmong American Writing: "How Do I Begin?" "Our Fields," "Hunger," "In My Fresno Backyard," "Afternoon at the Long Cheng Café," "The Last Drops," "In the End"

Bamboo Among the Oaks: Contemporary Writing by Hmong Americans: "A Tropical Garden in the San Joaquin Valley," "Chino," "Letter from the Shore of the Dragon River," "Immunization," "Retired," and "The American"

How Much Earth: The Fresno Poets: "Letter from the Shore of the Dragon River," "A Tropical Garden in the San Joaquin Valley"

Tilting the Continent: Southeast Asian American Literature: "My War with Slugs"

The Packinghouse Review: "A Love Poem"

In the Grove: "Afternoon at the Long Cheng Café"

Paj Ntaub Voice: "A Tropical Garden in the San Joaquin Valley," "Chino," "Letter from the Shore of the Dragon River," "Immunization," "In My Fresno Backyard," "The American," "Name Change," "Other Asian"

Central California Poetry Journal: "Chino"

Notes

The Last Sky: Long Cheng or Clear Valley, CIA code-named Sky Base, fell in May 14, 1975. A few thousand Hmong were airlifted to Thailand; the rest fled through jungles, evading capture or massacre to cross the Mekong in any way they could. The exodus took many years, in many waves.

Monsoon Season, Colors, The Battle are set in the refugee camp at Nong Khai, Thailand. At first, a barbed-wired pasture where refugees built shanties out of whatever scraps they could find. Wells and outhouses stood side by side beside the shanties. A more permanent camp was built later.

The Old Capital of Laos was Luang Prabang—the city of the Lao king; now a city of faded structures, some dating back to French colonial era.

Our Fields: Hmong historical information cited from: "Chinese Odyssey…" by Yuepheng L. Xiong, www.hmongnet.org/hmong-au/chmong.htm

Love & War: The general had multiple wives living in a compound built by the CIA based on the Motel 6 design. During the war, he recalled that he was always on stand-by 24 hours a day to respond to any outbreak of battle.

South of the Cloud is the meaning of Yunnan, where Sauropod dinosaur skeletons were discovered.

Afternoon at the Long Cheng Café: Long Cheng was a military base where the Hmong army, supplied and trained by the CIA, was headquartered. It was also an educational and cultural center for the Hmong.

Sky Soldier on a Mountaintop: Sky soldier/lord refers to the term "Cao Fa." They were freedom fighters that waged a guerrilla war against the communist government that came into power in 1975.

The Special Forces Soldier I Met on the Trail: White Star were U.S. Special Forces teams that trained "natives" in the use of weapons in Laos.

Ulenspiegel was a medieval German prankster who deflated the self-importance of townspeople and the nobility. It was also the name of a trendy pub in Giessen.

In My Fresno Backyard: After the Berlin Wall fell, former Iron Curtain countries open up to the West. Auschwitz, Poland is a concentration camp where Nazis exterminated Jews. The place still stands, with barracks, gas chambers, and piles of shoes, clothing, and hair belonging to the Jews.

In the Jungle: After the U. S. left, communists took over Laos and brought in Russian and Cuban advisors. Some of them encountered Cao Fa guerillas in the jungle.

©Bob Marcotte

Soul Vang is the author of *To Live Here*, winner of the 2014 Imaginary Friend Press Poetry Prize and co-editor of *How Do I Begin?: A Hmong American Literary Anthology* (Heyday, 2011).

Soul is a poet, teacher, and U.S. Army veteran. He holds an MFA in poetry from California State University, Fresno and is an editorial board member of the Hmong American Writers' Circle (HAWC).

His writing has appeared in *Fiction Attic Press*, *In the Grove*, *The Packinghouse Review*, *Southeast Asia Globe*, and *The New York Times*, among others.

His poetry has been anthologized in *Tilting the Continent: Southeast Asian American Writing* (New Rivers), *How Much Earth: An Anthology of Fresno Poets* (Roundhouse), *Bamboo Among the Oaks: Contemporary Writing by Hmong Americans* (Minnesota Historical Society), *How Do I Begin? A Hmong American Literary Anthology* (Heyday), and *NEW CALIFORNIA WRITING 2012* (Heyday).